ALL OF A SUDDEN AND FOREVER

HELP AND HEALING AFTER THE OKLAHOMA CITY BOMBING

CHRIS BARTON

ILLUSTRATIONS BY NICOLE XU

Carolrhoda Books

Minneapolis

For Declan Asher Barton
—C.B.

For my mom
—N.X.

Sometimes bad things happen, and you have to tell everyone.

Sometimes terrible things happen, and everybody *knows*.

One April morning in 1995, one of those terrible things happened in Oklahoma City. There was a man with a bomb in a big truck.

He parked the truck in front of a big building in the middle of the city. He walked away.

One hundred sixty-eight people died.

All of a sudden—and forever—so much was ruined.

The awfulness of that moment can never be undone.

But the awfulness of that moment is not the end of the story.

It is true that many people were hurt,
in many, many ways.

Some lost a cousin, a niece, a nephew, an uncle,
an aunt, a grandfather, a grandmother, a sister,
a brother, a mother, a father, a daughter, a son,
a baby named but not yet born.

Some lost friends, neighbors, folks they used to
see every week or every day.

It is true, as well, that some who
survived had their bodies broken
in ways large and small.

Some suffered damage to their
minds and spirits.

Some, who rushed in to help,
saw horrible things they would
never forget.

Some had to leave nearby places they loved—homes, churches,
a library—without knowing when they could safely return.

And it is true that some found their lives flooded with anger, grief, or fear.

Some came under suspicion for no good reason.

Some had to accept that their own child was a bomber or had kept secrets for someone who was.

Some lost hope that anything would ever be okay again.

Many, many people around the world watched
the tragedy and felt their own hearts break.

And then, not all at once but one by one,
they turned to look at other things instead.

But it is also true that, all the while, one tree stood near the bombed building.

This tree, an American elm, had not been much to look at before the bombing, though it did give off some shade.

The blast had scorched the elm, blown debris into its branches, and left it looking worse than ever.

Investigators collecting evidence considered
cutting down the tree, but it was spared.

It received help.

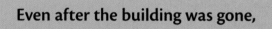

Even after the building was gone,

the tree survived.

During the next year, people dealt with their pain in different ways.
But healing doesn't always come easily.

Many whose lives had been changed by the bombing asked why.

Why me?

Why us?

Why them?

Why?

While waiting for an answer that may never come, many vowed to remember. They vowed to tell their stories.

Their stories would keep alive those they had lost. Those stories, told and retold, would make sure the past had a place in the present.

Many learned to piece their lives back together, even when important parts were gone forever. Some needed lots of help, and they received it from lots of people.

Some of those helpers themselves were hurting—maybe from the bombing, maybe from something else that had happened to them before. Helpers often know how it feels to be in need, and they know from their own difficult times what kinds of aid might be needed.

Families, survivors, and helpers came together. They talked, they listened, they cried, and sometimes even laughed. They fixed— they made right—what they could and began looking to the future. Some took solace under that elm tree that had survived.

When the next spring came and new seeds fell from the Survivor Tree's branches, someone thought to collect them. Something could be done with those.

The seeds were taken to a nursery where helpers planted
them—not all at once but a few seeds at a time.

While the seeds sprouted and grew, so did plans for a memorial at the place of the bombing.

It would be a monument to what had been lost but also to the community of those still living. None of them had been hurt in exactly the same way, yet they all could seek some healing in this space they had in common.

As time went by, they each might encounter others in their lives—on occasion, or every morning— ready for them to just move on. To stop being sad. To stop being angry. To stop being hurt.

At the memorial site, they believed, they would always find
someone willing to listen. They could always find someone
willing to be with them.

This was especially true each anniversary. When they gathered
there for the second one, they found more than listeners,
friends, and loved ones. They found Survivor Tree seedlings,
grown from the seeds harvested the previous spring.

There were enough seedlings for families of those who had
died to take one home to plant.

In front yards and backyards where everyday comings and goings mixed with memories from before the bombing, those seedlings took root and started to grow.

Sometimes those elm trees were reminders of loss. Sometimes they were sources of comfort. Sometimes they were both.

Many people whose lives had been changed by the bombing found new connections with each other.

These included friendships, other close relationships, and at least one marriage that never would have happened if not for that terrible something they wished had never happened at all.

After five years, the memorial opened to the public, followed by a museum. The stories they told brought visitors from around the world.

A new crop of seeds got collected each spring. Over the next year, they would sprout into seedlings. At the anniversary gathering the following April, those seedlings would go to more homes, farther and farther from the original Survivor Tree.

And when other terrible things happened—

They just do. We can't stop them all.

When these other terrible things happened, and people died or were hurt or had their lives changed—all of a sudden and forever—they received help too.

Sometimes, that help came from Oklahoma City.

Some of those who had needed so much help after the bombing—
even some of those who still needed help themselves—came forward.
They provided comfort to those hurting in other families, other cities,
other states, other nations.

They listened to the stories of others. They shared their own. And
before they returned home to Oklahoma City, sometimes they left
behind a reminder of that comfort. Sometimes, they left behind a
seedling from the Survivor Tree.

There will come a time—many, many years from now—when those people whose lives changed the instant of the Oklahoma City bombing will no longer be with us. Not all at once, but as decades pass, they will be gone.

Likewise, the Survivor Tree itself will not live forever. No tree ever does.

But its seedlings have been planted near and far. Those have grown into trees that have given off their own seeds. And just as the Survivor Tree's offspring have spread, so has the story of the tree and its survival. In various ways, this one tree with a meaningful place in our past will always be with us.

The same is true of the people who first took solace from the Survivor Tree. After they are gone, some of those they comforted will remain among us, continuing to comfort others . . .

who themselves will comfort still others . . .

who will be around to comfort still more.

And because of the stories so many of us have shared . . .

We will remember the help so many needed.

We will remember the help so many received.

We will remember the help so many provided.

We will remember.

Author's Note

All of a Sudden and Forever began in 2016 with an unplanned stop at the Oklahoma City National Memorial & Museum during a trip to visit Oklahoma schools. Before that day, I had seen photographs of the field of empty chairs representing the 168 people killed in the 1995 bombing of the Alfred P. Murrah Federal Building, but I had never been to the memorial in person. And I had no idea that there was a museum.

That brief visit gave me a better understanding of the tragedy. It also gave me a sense of how the effects of that terrorist attack—some public, many private—continued to unfold. Long after I got home, the stories told by the Memorial & Museum would not let me go. They resonated with me so strongly that I knew I wanted to write a book, though I did not yet know what I wanted to say.

I began to research the bombing. I learned about some of the different paths people took as they tried to recover from that horrible event, and about the role played by the creation of the Memorial. I returned to Oklahoma City, spoke with staff members of the Memorial & Museum, and explored the archives. I read many books and articles about the bombing and watched a handful of documentary movies.

I reached out to several survivors, first responders, family members of victims, and others I believed might have insights that could benefit the young people I write for. The conversations that resulted led to my decision to focus this book on those I interviewed and others like them. I am grateful to those who took the time to talk with me, and I appreciate those who chose to tend to their own well-being rather than be interviewed by a stranger about the worst time in their lives.

Whether I spoke with them or not, I hope that my text—joined with Nicole Xu's thoughtful, tender, and beautiful art—has succeeded in honoring their experiences as well as the deep capacity for informed empathy among my readers.

The Alfred P. Murrah Federal Building in the late 1970s.

The Survivor Tree in 1996. Behind it is the Journal Record Building, which now houses the Oklahoma City National Memorial Museum.

All of a Sudden and Forever was mostly finished when, on April 19, 2019, I visited Oklahoma City. This was my third trip to the Oklahoma City National Memorial & Museum during my making of this book, but it was a first in some important ways.

I was joined by my wife, Jennifer Ziegler, as well as by this book's editor, Carol Hinz, and its art director, Danielle Carnito, the first time any of them had been to the Memorial & Museum. It was—on the twenty-fourth anniversary of the 1995 bombing—the first time I had attended the annual Remembrance Ceremony. And it was the first time I had met in person with any of the survivors or the victims' family members that I had previously interviewed by phone.

My research should have prepared me for the sense of community among those I had come to see and among others with similar experiences. And I suppose that it *had* prepared me. Amid the sorrow, there was joy, just as one might expect at a funeral attended by family members happy to be reunited despite the circumstances.

Yet like the rest of my group, I was struck by the extremes, by the intensity of the lows and highs, of both the sadness and the gladness. Nearly a quarter century after the tragedy, the powerful emotions it evokes were still very close to the surface for these people and in this place.

By contrast, the names of those who committed this crime barely came up during our visit. Their identities are not secret. Those interested in learning about them can do so within seconds, but their stories are not among those that I have chosen to tell.

None of us is immune to tragedy, be it in our families, in our communities, or shared throughout our nation and beyond. In researching and writing *All of a Sudden and Forever*, I have tried to convey aspects of the journeys of Oklahoma City bombing survivors, victims' families, and others whose lives were altered dramatically on April 19, 1995. My hope is that as new tragedies enter our lives, or as we grapple with past losses, we can take some comfort from the experiences and efforts of those who have traveled a difficult road and gained some perspective on their own journey.

The Survivor Tree in May 2014

Illustrator's Note

When I first read the manuscript of *All of a Sudden and Forever*, I was overwhelmed with feelings of sorrow and awe. I was excited to work on the project but also incredibly scared at the prospect. How was I going to create imagery that befitted Chris Barton's words?

I confess that at the time, I did not know much about the Oklahoma City bombing. When the tragedy occurred, I was on the other side of the world, in China, oblivious to everything as a four-month-old baby. To make up for my lack of knowledge, I pored over Chris's research and read as many materials as I could find.

For me, the key to understanding it all was reading interviews with survivors and loved ones of the victims. Those gave me the perspective I needed to empathize, and they provided the inspiration I needed to tell their story.

After reading the interviews, I started working on the sketches. I knew that the mood of the art was going to be the aspect I wanted to focus on, so the first thing I did was fill in the white pages with the colors that reflected the tone of the writing. After that was done, I started adding in the layers of people, buildings, and trees. I knew that I wanted to add in textures to the pieces as well, so I used ink to stain some papers, scanned the papers, and arranged them on the art.

Toward the end of the project, while I was finishing my illustrations, I got the chance to visit the Oklahoma City National Memorial & Museum, thanks to the generosity of my partner, Tyler, and his parents, Melinda and Bob Wilbers. The Memorial Museum was such an immersive experience, and being there in person gave me a deeper understanding of something I had previously only read about. When I got home, I went back into the art and added many of the details that were missing before.

I'm extremely grateful to have the opportunity to work on this project, and I hope that it will bring a degree of comfort to those who need it.

Research Materials and Interview Subjects

The author's research for this book included interviews with the people listed below, as well as with members of the administration and staff of the Oklahoma City National Memorial & Museum. You can find the complete list of interviewees and bibliography of other sources consulted at https://www.chrisbarton.info/books/okc.html.

Catherine Alaniz-Simonds and Keith Simonds

Catherine Alaniz was widowed at the age of nineteen when her first husband died during Operation Desert Storm in 1991. Four years later, her father, customs agent Claude Medearis, was killed in the Murrah bombing. In 1997 she was on her way to Denver to testify in a federal trial related to the bombing when she met fellow witness Keith Simonds, an Oklahoma City police officer who had been a first responder on April 19, 1995. They fell in love and in 2000 were married beneath the Survivor Tree.

Mark Bays

Mark Bays, an urban forestry coordinator with Oklahoma Forestry Services, has helped lead efforts to revive, preserve, and propagate the Survivor Tree since shortly after the Murrah bombing.

G. Keith Bryant

Keith Bryant was a thirty-five-year veteran of the Oklahoma City Fire Department when he retired as chief in 2017 to become the US fire administrator for the Federal Emergency Management Agency. He has also chaired the Oklahoma City National Memorial Conscience Committee, which provides an ongoing voice for survivors, victims' families, and first responders in the operations of the Memorial and Museum.

John Cole

John Cole's godsons Aaron and Elijah Coverdale were among the children killed in the Murrah Building's day care center. He served as a member of the design selection committee for the Oklahoma City National Memorial as well as on the National Memorial's board of directors.

Constance Favorite

Constance Favorite's daughter, Air Force Airman First Class Lakesha Levy, died in the Murrah bombing. After the United States was attacked on September 11, 2001, Favorite went to New York to comfort families of victims killed in the World Trade Center towers.

Deb Ferrell-Lynn

Deb Ferrell-Lynn's cousin Susan Ferrell was an attorney for the US Department of Housing and Urban Development when she was killed in the bombing. Ferrell-Lynn served on the Oklahoma City National Memorial's Board of Trustees and was paired with Constance Favorite while consoling families of 9/11 victims.

Dot Hill

Dot Hill worked on the first floor of the Murrah Building. She has since been active in efforts to support survivors and others affected by terrorism in Oklahoma City, New York, and elsewhere.

Gary Knight

Gary Knight, a patrolman for the Oklahoma City Police Department, happened to be about 150 yards (137 m) from the Murrah Building at the time of the explosion. He was among the first to begin helping those injured by the blast. Knight went on to become a master sergeant and an assistant public information officer with the department.

Ken Thompson

Ken Thompson's mother, Virginia Thompson, worked for the Federal Employees Credit Union and was the last victim of the Murrah bombing to be identified, forty-three days after the blast. He was heavily involved in the creation and operation of the Oklahoma City National Memorial and in providing comfort and guidance following other terrorist attacks.

Susan Walton

Susan Walton was at the Murrah Building to make a deposit at the credit union when the bomb exploded. Recovery from her injuries included more than two dozen surgeries. Along the way, she began Suited for Success, a nonprofit organization that has provided clothing for around ten thousand women.

Richard Williams

Richard Williams was the assistant manager of the Murrah Building, and the explosion buried him in rubble. While recovering from his injuries, he worked on creating the National Memorial's mission statement. Since then, he has planted Survivor Trees and spoken about his experiences to student groups in several states.

Recommended Reading

Blanco, Richard. *One Today*. Illustrated by Dav Pilkey. New York: Little, Brown, 2015.

Bunting, Eve. *The Wall*. Illustrated by Ronald Himler. New York: Clarion Books, 1990.

Clifton, Lucille. *Everett Anderson's Goodbye*. Illustrated by Ann Grifalconi. New York: Henry Holt, 1983.

Deedy, Carmen Agra. With Wilson Kimeli Naiyomah. *14 Cows for America*. Illustrated by Thomas Gonzalez. Atlanta: Peachtree, 2009.

Drummond, Allan. *Green City: How One Community Survived a Tornado and Rebuilt for a Sustainable Future*. New York: Farrar Straus Giroux, 2016.

Gralley, Jean. *The Moon Came Down on Milk Street*. New York: Henry Holt, 2004.

Kalman, Maira. *Fireboat: The Heroic Adventures of the* John J. Harvey. New York: G. P. Putnam's Sons, 2002.

Paul, Michael G. *Oklahoma City and Anti-Government Terrorism*. Milwaukee: World Almanac Library, 2006.

Perkins, Lynne Rae. *The Broken Cat*. New York: Greenwillow Books, 2002.

Reul, Sarah Lynne. *The Breaking News*. New York: Roaring Brook, 2018.

Robison, Brad. *If the Fence Could Talk*. Illustrated by Margaret Hoge. Oklahoma City: Oklahoma Heritage Association, 2015.

Scanlon, Liz Garton. *All the World*. Illustrated by Marla Frazee. New York: Beach Lane Books, 2009.

Sherrow, Victoria. *Homegrown Terror: The Oklahoma City Bombing*. Berkeley Heights, NJ: Enslow, 2013.

Other Recommended Resources

The Oklahoma City National Memorial & Museum
https://oklahomacitynationalmemorial.org

9/11 Memorial & Museum
https://www.911memorial.org/

The National Child Traumatic Stress Network
https://www.nctsn.org/

Carolrhoda Books®
An imprint of Lerner Publishing Group, Inc.
241 First Avenue North
Minneapolis, MN 55401 USA

For reading levels and more information, look up this title at www.lernerbooks.com.

Photos: Courtesy of the LWPB Architects and Planners Collection, Oklahoma City National Memorial & Museum, p. 36 (top); CHRIS WILKINS/AFP/Getty Images, p. 36 (bottom); DIANE COOK, LEN JENSHEL/Alamy Stock Photo, p. 37.

Designed by Danielle Carnito.
Main body text set in Cronos Pro Semibold. Typeface provided by Adobe Systems.
The illustrations in this book were created with ink and Photoshop.

Library of Congress Cataloging-in-Publication Data

Names: Barton, Chris, author. | Xu, Nicole, 1994– illustrator.
Title: All of a sudden and forever : help and healing after the Oklahoma City bombing / Chris Barton ; illustrated by Nicole Xu.
Description: Minneapolis : Carolrhoda Books, [2020] | Includes bibliographical references.
Identifiers: LCCN 2018047653 (print) | LCCN 2018051277 (ebook) | ISBN 9781541560987 (eb pdf) | ISBN 9781541526693 (lb : alk. paper)
Subjects: LCSH: Oklahoma City Federal Building Bombing, Oklahoma City, Okla., 1995—Juvenile literature. | Victims of terrorism—Oklahoma—Oklahoma City—Juvenile literature.
Classification: LCC HV6432.6 (ebook) | LCC HV6432.6 .B37 2020 (print) | DDC 363.325/140976638—dc23

LC record available at https://lccn.loc.gov/2018047653

Manufactured in the United States of America
1-44610-35513-6/19/2019